The Forest

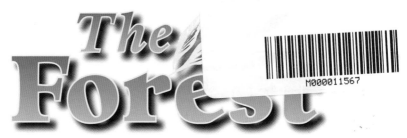

Kimberly Kern

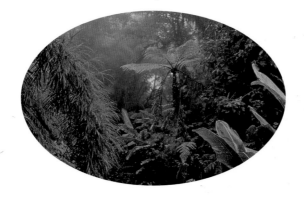

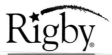

A Harcourt Achieve Imprint

www.Rigby.com
1-800-531-5015

Here is a tree.

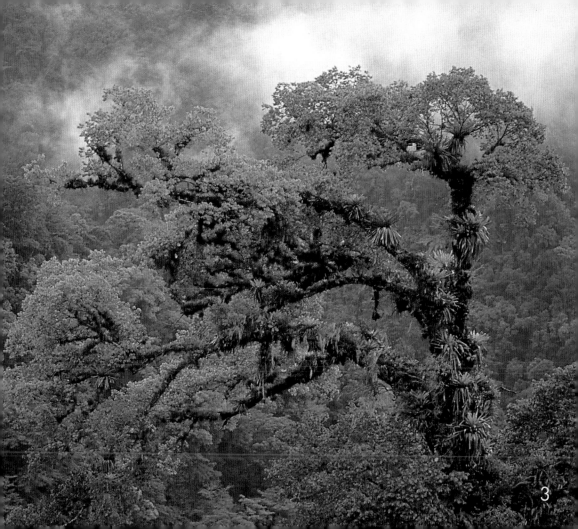

Here is a bird.

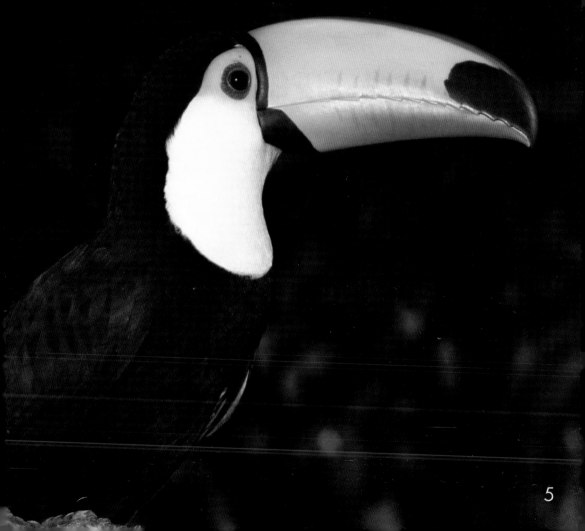

Here is a frog.

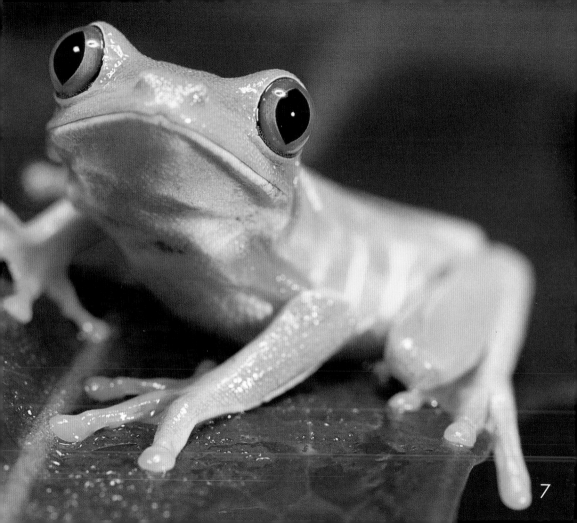

Here is a spider.

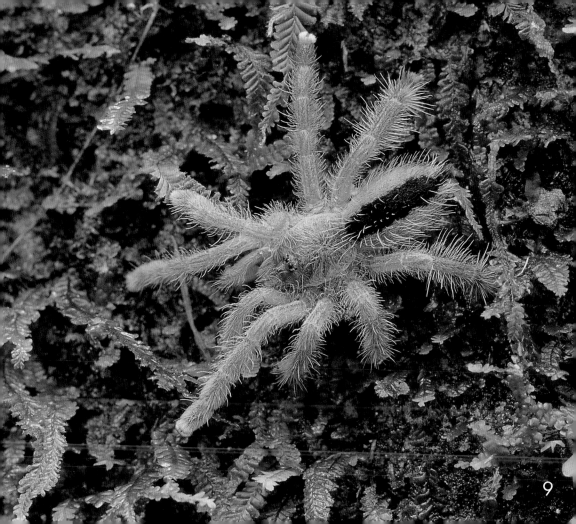

Here is a lizard.

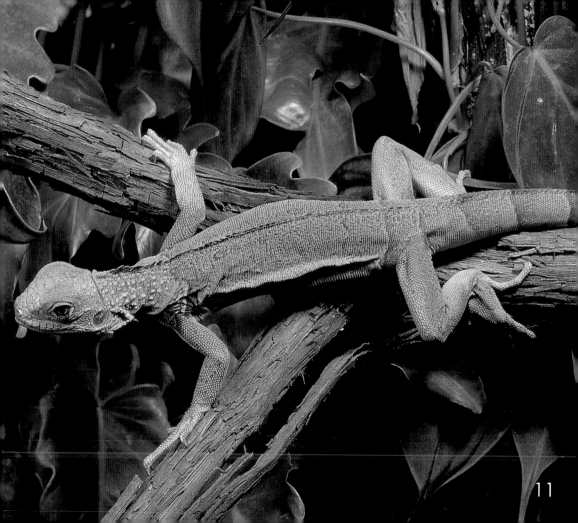

Here is a snake.

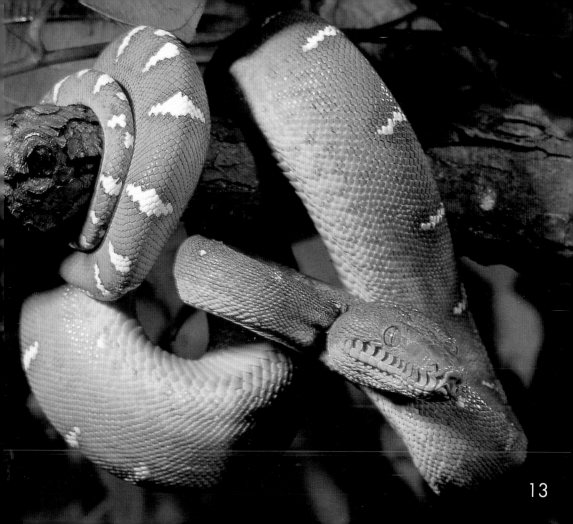

Here is a monkey.

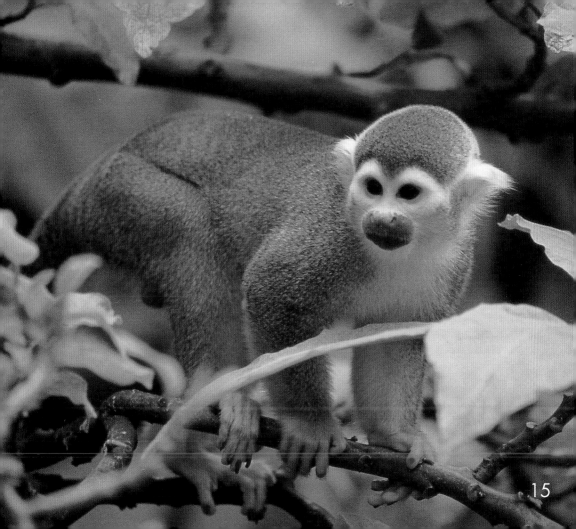

Here is a forest.

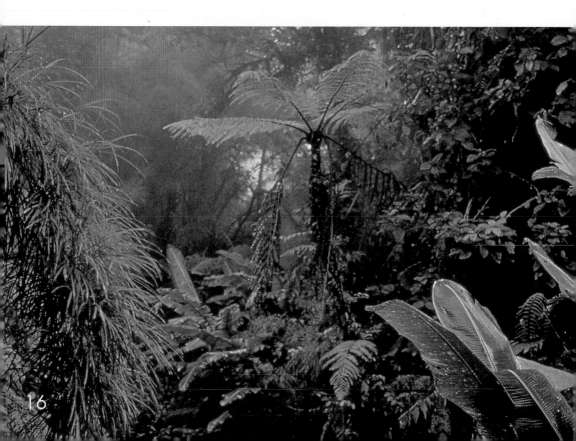